The Promise of His Presence

16 Weeks of Finding God
in the Midst of Suffering

Hilda H. McClure, LPC

Dedication

To my abuelita Hilda, who carried her great suffering with grace, letting it soften her heart and make her tender, compassionate, and endlessly loving. You taught me how to see every soul as worthy of God's grace and love, and how to root myself in a deep, abiding love for Him.

I rise up and call you blessed.

A mi abuelita Hilda, que llevó su sufrimiento con gracia, permitiendo que suavizara su corazón y lo llenara de ternura, compasión y un amor infinito. Me enseñaste a contemplar cada alma como digna de la gracia y el amor de Dios, y a enraizarme en un amor profundo y constante por Él.

Me pongo de pie y te proclamo bendecida.

How to Use This Devotional

This devotional is designed as a six-day weekly rhythm to help you engage deeply with scripture, your inner life, and God's presence. Each week focuses on one passage and its accompanying reflections, guiding you through reading, prayer, contemplation, creativity, community, and rest. The structure is intentional: it moves from personal reflection to theological depth, creative exploration, relational practice, and finally, restorative rest.

General Guidelines for Use

Pace yourself:
Each day's practice is flexible—complete it in one sitting or spread it across the day.

Journaling:
Strongly encouraged, but optional. Writing helps integrate insights and track growth.

Presence over performance:
The goal is not perfection or productivity. Engage honestly with your experience.

Repeat and revisit:
Some practices may resonate more than others. Return to them as needed.

Adapt to your context:
Modify practices to your life and energy levels. Creativity, prayer, or service may look different for each person.

Be curious:
Not everything I offer here is a good fit for you. You may not even come to the same conclusions as I did. I would invite you to think deeper about your own conclusions and what God is revealing to you personally.

This is not one size fits all:
You may not enjoy the specific practices or exercises I offer here. That's okay. Try something different that allows you to dig deeper with the Lord. The bigger picture is that we engage with God and His Word, and let it move and impact us in ways that produce holiness in us.

This devotional is designed to guide you into deeper awareness of God, your own heart, and the ways the Spirit moves in ordinary life and in suffering. Approach it with curiosity, patience, and openness.

Weekly Structure

Day 1 – Reading & Personal Reflection

Begin by reading the Scripture passage and the devotional. Don't rush. Allow the words to settle in. Take note of your first impressions, emotions, and questions. This is your initial encounter with God's Word, before analysis or interpretation. Consider journaling: What stands out to you? Which words or phrases stir your heart? What personal experiences or emotions arise as you read?

Day 2 – Contemplative Prayer

On this day, you are invited into listening and presence with God. Set aside 10–20 minutes in a quiet space. You may sit, lie down, or walk gently. Begin by breathing deeply, slowly inhaling and exhaling. Then, bring the week's Scripture or devotional to mind. Speak to God honestly, or simply be silent. The key is to allow space for God to speak, and for your heart to receive. You may notice thoughts, images, emotions, or a sense of God's nearness. Journaling afterwards can help capture insights, but don't feel pressured. The goal is to practice being in His Presence.

Day 3 – Deeper Thoughts / Reflection

Today invites you into intellectual and spiritual exploration. You will encounter a set of questions designed to dig beneath the surface of the Scripture and devotional. Engage thoughtfully, wrestling with meaning, theology, and personal application. This is an opportunity to explore your beliefs, challenge assumptions, and grow in understanding. Journaling or discussing these questions with a trusted friend can deepen your insight.

Day 4 – Creative Expression

Creativity is a pathway to encounter God beyond words. On this day, respond to the Scripture and devotional through an expressive practice: writing poetry or a letter to God, sketching, making music, moving, or any form that helps your heart process and reflect. Don't worry too much about skill. The goal is to experience your inner life and God's presence in a tangible, embodied way.

Day 5 – Community & Service

Faith is never fully realized in isolation. Today, the practice is relational: seek ways to share, serve, or connect with others. You might pray for someone, offer encouragement, participate in a service project, or simply listen to a friend. These actions remind us that God works through community and that our spiritual growth is intertwined with the lives of those around us. Reflect on how your experiences of this week could translate into compassionate action or shared encouragement.

Day 6 – Rest Practice

The week concludes with intentional rest, reflection, and Sabbath practice. Reflect on the insights, emotions, and growth of the week. Notice where God was present, even in struggle or silence. You might spend time journaling, meditating, walking in nature, or engaging in quiet reflection. This day is about surrender, gratitude, and renewal, allowing God's presence to permeate your being. Resting is an active spiritual practice: it's an acknowledgment that God's work is ongoing, even when we pause.

The Breath of God

"When God created man, He formed him out of dust and then breathed His breath into him. Adam's first breath was the breath of God—the first sign that we belong to Him."

>

"This is the account of the heavens and the earth when they were created. When the Lord God made the earth and the heavens, no shrub of the field had yet appeared on the earth and no plant of the field had yet sprung up, for the Lord God had not sent rain on the earth and there was no one to work the ground, but streams came up from the earth and watered the whole surface of the ground. Then the Lord God formed a man from the dust of the ground and breathed into his nostrils the breath of life, and the man became a living being."

Genesis 2:4–7

"Moses said to God, 'Suppose I go to the Israelites and say to them, "The God of your fathers has sent me to you," and they ask me, "What is his name?" Then what shall I tell them?' God said to Moses, 'I AM WHO I AM. This is what you are to say to the Israelites: "I AM has sent me to you."' God also said to Moses, 'Say to the Israelites, "The Lord, the God of your fathers—the God of Abraham, the God of Isaac and the God of Jacob—has sent me to you." This is my name forever, the name you shall call me from generation to generation.'"

Exodus 3:13–15

We're first introduced to God's name Yahweh in Genesis 2:4. It comes from the Hebrew root meaning "I Am." Later, in Exodus 3, when God sends Moses to Pharaoh, He declares, "I AM WHO I AM." In Hebrew, it's written as YHWH—a tetragrammaton, meaning "four letters."

The name itself is mysterious. It has no vowels, so its exact pronunciation is unknown. It was considered so sacred that scribes weren't allowed to stop writing once they began it. Over time, it was replaced by Adonai or other titles for God, out of reverence for His holiness. In the process, also forgetting the
pronunciation. Yahweh reveals God's character as all-encompassing, self-existent, and self-sufficient—yet deeply personal, used especially when He made covenant with His people.
(It's worth studying—there's such rich depth in that name.)

There is a school of thought that the letters are aspirated consonants—meaning they represent breathing sounds.

Inhale—Yah.
Exhale—weh.

I wonder if that's on purpose.

When God created man, He formed him out of dust and then breathed His breath into him. Adam's first breath was the breath of God—the first sign that we belong to Him. He is so close to us that He is literally a breath away.
There are days when there aren't enough words to describe the pain, the hurt, the disappointment. And other days, there are no words at all—just groanings. Yet in His kindness, God gives us His own breath to remind us that He is near.
As you embark on this journey, beloved, as you inhale and exhale, you utter His name.

And that is enough.
He is near — as near as your breath.

Reading & Personal Reflection

Read the Scriptures and the devotional. Write down your first thoughts.

Ask yourself:
What part of this passage or reflection stands out most to me?

How do I feel God's presence in my own breath or body today?

Is there a part of me resisting or longing to connect with God right now?

_____

_____

_____

_____

_____

_____

_____

_____

_____

_____

_____

_____

"Yahweh,
You are the breath that fills my lungs,
the whisper between my inhale and exhale.
When I am wordless, You speak for me.
When I am weary, You breathe life again.
Let every breath remind me that You are
here—closer than I can comprehend,
faithful beyond what I can see.
May I rest in the mystery of Your name:
I Am — ever present, ever near.
Amen."

2

Contemplative Prayer

Sit quietly, breathe deeply, and read the prayer slowly. Pause to reflect, notice your thoughts and feelings, and rest in God's presence.

Deeper Reflection

Take a moment to dig deeper into these vereses and answer the questions below:

What does it mean that God's name, Yahweh, translates to "I Am"? How does that challenge or comfort your view of His nature?

Why do you think God chose to reveal Himself as I Am Who I Am—a name that emphasizes being rather than doing?

How might understanding God as breath (sustaining life moment by moment) reshape how you experience His presence in suffering?

Write a short poem or journal entry where each line begins with
"I breathe and remember…"

Record a 1-minute voice memo of your breathing while reciting
"Yah—weh."

Consider movement or dance—simply flow with your breath,
imagining God's Spirit moving with you.

4

Creative Practice

Create something that helps you meditate on the Scripture and devotional.

Community & Service

Consider someone in your life who feels like they're "in the pit."

Send a short message, offer a quiet presence, or drop off something that says, "You're not alone."

Reflect on your ideas, make a plan and do it.
How did you feel after you served that person?

_____
_____
_____
_____
_____
_____
_____
_____
_____
_____
_____
_____
_____
_____

Find a quiet space.

Close your eyes and begin to notice your breath.
As you inhale, whisper "Yah."
As you exhale, whisper "Weh."

Stay here for a few minutes.

When your mind wanders, gently return to the sound of His name.
Let your whole being rest in the truth:
He is near, even here.

6

Rest Practice

The Twenty-Four Elders

"We shy away from discomfort—even in small ways—because it's hard, inconvenient, or unpleasant. And yet, these elders endured and remained faithful."

>

4 "Then as I looked, I saw a door standing open in heaven, and the same voice I had heard before spoke to me like a trumpet blast. The voice said, "Come up here, and I will show you what must happen after this." 2 And instantly I was in the Spirit,[a] and I saw a throne in heaven and someone sitting on it. 3 The one sitting on the throne was as brilliant as gemstones—like jasper and carnelian. And the glow of an emerald circled his throne like a rainbow. 4 Twenty-four thrones surrounded him, and twenty-four elders sat on them. They were all clothed in white and had gold crowns on their heads. 5 From the throne came flashes of lightning and the rumble of thunder. And in front of the throne were seven torches with burning flames. This is the sevenfold Spirit[b] of God. 6 In front of the throne was a shiny sea of glass, sparkling like crystal. In the center and around the throne were four living beings, each covered with eyes, front and back. 7 The first of these living beings was like a lion; the second was like an ox; the third had a human face; and the fourth was like an eagle in flight. 8 Each of these living beings had six wings, and their wings were covered all over with eyes, inside and out. Day after day and night after night they keep on saying, "Holy, holy, holy is the Lord God, the Almighty— the one who always was, who is, and who is still to come."9 Whenever the living beings give glory and honor and thanks to the one sitting on the throne (the one who lives forever and ever), 10 the twenty-four elders fall down and worship the one sitting on the throne (the one who lives forever and ever). And they lay their crowns before the throne and say,11 "You are worthy, O Lord our God, to receive glory and honor and power. For you created all things, and they exist because you created what you pleased."

Revelation 4:1 - 11

In Revelation 4, John sees 24 elders in white robes surrounding the throne. It's commonly believed they represent the 12 leaders of the Old Testament Church (the sons of Judah) and the 12 leaders of the New Testament Church (the apostles). At the end of the chapter, they fall before God, casting their crowns at His feet, saying:

"Worthy are You, our Lord and our God, to receive glory and honor and power; for You created all things, and because of Your will they existed and were created."

A chapter later, another image unfolds. This time it's not just the elders—it's a multitude no one could count, also dressed in white. When John asks who they are, one of the elders replies: they are the ones who've come out of the great tribulation. The ones who've endured. Who've washed their robes in the blood of the Lamb and now serve God day and night.

What strikes me about both these groups—the 24 elders and the great multitude—is their intimacy with suffering. Most of the apostles were martyred. But I imagine they also carried the weight of quieter sorrows: family estrangement, aching loneliness, the grief of losing beloved friends and co-laborers. Even knowing Jesus had risen, I wonder if they missed His nearness in the way it existed before. Did they ever feel abandoned? Did the glory they preached ever feel impossibly far?

And still—they worship anyway.

I think about them often - they had every reason to withhold their praise. And chose not to. This leads me to the thought if they worship despite their suffering, God really is Who He says He is. We shy away from
discomfort—even in small ways—because it's hard, inconvenient, or unpleasant. And yet, these elders endured and remained faithful.

What motivates such perseverance? Love. A deep, unwavering trust in someone whose goodness and faithfulness are undeniable.

The 24 elders declare Jesus worthy because He is exactly who He says He is—a loving, faithful, and generous presence. He carried, protected, and cared for them.

As we walk through our own challenges, we can take comfort in this truth: God is who He says He is. His death and resurrection confirm it. And even in the midst of suffering, He is worthy of our trust, our devotion, and our hearts.

Reading & Personal Reflection

Read the Scriptures and the devotional. Write down your first thoughts.

Ask yourself:
What part of this passage or reflection stands out most to me?

Do I believe He is worthy of my trust in suffering? Why or why not?

Is there a part of me resisting or longing to connect with God right now?

_____
_____
_____
_____
_____
_____
_____
_____
_____
_____
_____
_____
_____
_____

Jesus,
Even when life is hard, and my heart aches,
I choose to lay my crowns at Your feet.
Teach me to trust in Your faithfulness,
to honor You not for what You do,
but for who You are.

When I am weary, remind me of the elders' example — that love and devotion endure even through suffering.

Help me rest in the certainty of Your goodness,
and to say, simply: You are worthy.
Amen.

2 Contemplative Prayer

Sit quietly, breathe deeply, and read the prayer slowly. Pause to reflect, notice your thoughts and feelings, and rest in God's presence.

Deeper Reflection

Take a moment to dig deeper into these vereses and answer the questions below:

Why do the elders in Revelation declare Jesus worthy despite their suffering?

What does this tell us about the nature of true worship?

How does acknowledging God's faithfulness—even when life is hard—affect the way we understand His character?

In what ways does perseverance through suffering deepen our love and trust in God compared to times of comfort?

___

___

___

___

___

___

___

___

___

___

___

___

___

Write a letter to Jesus describing the ways you've seen Him faithful in your own life, especially in times of difficulty.

Draw or collage a crown or other symbol of what you might "lay at His feet" as a representation of trust.

Compose a short prayer, poem, or song honoring God's faithfulness in the midst of struggle.

Find a song that helps you worship Him as worthy.

4

Creative Practice

Create something that helps you meditate on the Scripture and devotional.

Community & Service

Reach out to someone who is going through trials. Share a verse, a prayer, or just sit with them in silence, reminding them that Jesus is worthy even when life is hard.

Consider volunteering with a ministry or organization that supports those experiencing suffering or hardship this week.

Reflect on how your presence and encouragement can serve as a reminder of God's faithfulness to others.

_____
_____
_____
_____
_____
_____
_____
_____
_____
_____
_____
_____
_____
_____
_____

Sit quietly and reflect on the truth: God is who He says He is.
Close your eyes, breathe slowly, and whisper: "He is faithful."

Release the need to control outcomes.
Visualize laying your burdens, worries, and crowns at Jesus' feet.

Allow your heart to rest in the reality of His love and devotion,
knowing that even in suffering,

He is worthy—and near.

6

Rest Practice

Our High Priest

"Jesus goes beyond just empathy - feeling what we are feeling. He committed to not observing our pain from a distance. He enters it with us."

"

12 *"For the word of God is alive and powerful. It is sharper than the sharpest two-edged sword, cutting between soul and spirit, between joint and marrow. It exposes our innermost thoughts and desires.* 13 *Nothing in all creation is hidden from God. Everything is naked and exposed before his eyes, and he is the one to whom we are accountable.*

14 *So then, since we have a great High Priest who has entered heaven, Jesus the Son of God, let us hold firmly to what we believe.* 15 *This High Priest of ours understands our weaknesses, for he faced all of the same testings we do, yet he did not sin.* 16 *So let us come boldly to the throne of our gracious God. There we will receive his mercy, and we will find grace to help us when we need it most."*

Hebrews 4:12-16

Hebrews 2:17-18 states, "Therefore, it was necessary for him to be made in every respect like us, his brothers and sisters, so that he could be our merciful and faithful High Priest before God. Then he could offer a sacrifice that would take away the sins of the people. Since he himself has gone through suffering and testing, he is able to help us when we are being tested."

What if when the author mentions Jesus was made in every respect like us - He actually means that Jesus has the full experience of being human? He experienced hunger and thirst, sleepless nights, and physical exhaustion. He knew the sharp sting of betrayal, the ache of loneliness, and the weight of grief.

What if the mystery of incarnation is not just that He experienced humanity, but that He experienced it fully? He experienced it just like we do. He didn't bypass the struggles. He knew the discomfort of being misunderstood, the weight of the world's burdens, and the feeling of abandonment by his apostles and by God. He even asked, "My God, My God, what have you forsaken me?" The question many of us ask in our own suffering.

Jesus goes beyond just empathy - feeling what we are feeling. He committed to not observing our pain from a distance. He enters it with us. He endured suffering so He could meet us in ours, not just as a Savior, but as a companion who understands.

Don't miss this: He becomes our merciful and faithful High Priest, because He has lived the full experience of suffering. He advocates for us, and He helps us. He has a full understanding of our humanity in a deeply intimate way, and as a result, He can walk with us in our own suffering.

If you're suffering, you are not outside of God's reach. You are actually in the very place Jesus chose to meet humanity—in pain and heartbreak.
Jesus does not turn away from our pain. He draws near to it.
Not to fix us quickly, but to be with us fully.

His presence is the promise.
There is a unique invitation here not just to find comfort for ourselves,
but to become people who carry that same nearness into the pain of others.
May we be the people who do not run from pain - ours or anyone else's. To be the ones who sit beside the suffering, who do not flinch at sorrow, who refuse to rush past the ache.
Because we follow a Savior who chose proximity over power.
So let us be the ones who go there too.
Let us bear witness to one another's pain with gentleness and awe.
Let us become the kind of people who don't just say, "He gets it"—
but live as if that truth compels us to love more deeply, more patiently, more like Him.

May we remember that the margins of agony are not far from the presence of God. They are the place where He meets us.

Not just once.
Not just long ago.
Not when we have it all together.

But now.

Reading & Personal Reflection

Read the Scriptures and the devotional. Write down your first thoughts.

Ask yourself:
What part of this passage or reflection stands out most to me?

Where in my life do I need to remember that Jesus doesn't just observe my pain but enters it with me?

Is there a part of me resisting or longing to connect with God right now?

___
___
___
___
___
___
___
___
___
___
___
___
___
___
___

Jesus, our compassionate High Priest,
You know the depths of my heart,
every fear, every sorrow, every ordinary struggle.

You walked the paths I walk,
tempted, weary, yet without sin.

Let me approach Your throne with confidence,
resting not in my own strength, but in Your steadfast mercy and unchanging grace.

Teach me to receive Your compassion,
to dwell in Your presence, and to extend
that same love to others.

Hold me in my weakness,
guide me in my fear, and remind me that in You, I am fully known, fully held, fully loved.

Amen.

2

Contemplative Prayer

Sit quietly, breathe deeply, and read the prayer slowly. Pause to reflect, notice your thoughts and feelings, and rest in God's presence.

Deeper Reflection
Take a moment to dig deeper into these vereses and answer the questions below:

What does it mean for our faith that Jesus fully experienced both divine authority and human limitation? How does His humanity make Him approachable?

How does the knowledge that Jesus understands ordinary, daily struggles—like loneliness, frustration, or temptation—change your view of prayer and intercession?

2 Corinthians 1:3-4 suggests that our hardships can cultivate compassion for others. How have your own experiences prepared you to love, serve, and pray for people in ways you couldn't have otherwise?

___
___
___
___
___
___
___
___
___
___
___
___
___
___

Journal about a recent struggle, frustration, or temptation.
Then imagine Jesus walking through that exact moment with you—
how does He respond?
How does His presence shift your perspective?

Draw, sketch, or collage a representation of Jesus as your
intercessor, someone who stands in the gap, fully knowing your heart
and yet full of love.

If you prefer movement, consider pacing slowly or stretching while
breathing in His presence, imagining Him lifting the burdens from
your shoulders with every inhale and exhale.

4

Creative Practice
Create something that helps you meditate on the Scripture and devotional.

Community & Service

Identify someone in your life who is experiencing difficulty, whether emotional, spiritual, or physical. Write a note, call, or spend time with them, intentionally embodying Christ's empathy.

Reflect on ways your own experiences of struggle can inform your service. For example, if you've experienced loneliness, invite someone to coffee who has struggled with loneliness.

Pray specifically for those you serve: not just for their needs, but that they would encounter Jesus as a high priest who knows their heart fully.

Find a quiet space.

Close your eyes and begin with deep, slow breaths.
As you inhale, whisper: "He knows my heart."
As you exhale, imagine releasing control, fear, and shame.

Let the weight of your worries fall to the ground.

Reflect on the fullness of Jesus' empathy: He has lived the same ordinary human experiences you have, and yet intercedes for you with perfect love and justice.

Visualize yourself handing over the week's burdens to Him, one by one.

Let His presence soothe, sustain, and renew you.

6

Rest Practice

As Human as Peter

"But because of Jesus, we don't have to be afraid of God's presence. We can come to Him in our trembling and still find His hand reaching out to catch us."

"

22 "Immediately after this, Jesus insisted that his disciples get back into the boat and cross to the other side of the lake, while he sent the people home. 23 After sending them home, he went up into the hills by himself to pray. Night fell while he was there alone.

24 Meanwhile, the disciples were in trouble far away from land, for a strong wind had risen, and they were fighting heavy waves. 25 About three o'clock in the morning[b] Jesus came toward them, walking on the water. 26 When the disciples saw him walking on the water, they were terrified. In their fear, they cried out, "It's a ghost!"

27 But Jesus spoke to them at once. "Don't be afraid," he said. "Take courage. I am here![c]"

28 Then Peter called to him, "Lord, if it's really you, tell me to come to you, walking on the water."

29 "Yes, come," Jesus said.

So Peter went over the side of the boat and walked on the water toward Jesus. 30 But when he saw the strong[d] wind and the waves, he was terrified and began to sink. "Save me, Lord!" he shouted.

31 Jesus immediately reached out and grabbed him. "You have so little faith," Jesus said. "Why did you doubt me?"

32 When they climbed back into the boat, the wind stopped. 33 Then the disciples worshiped him. "You really are the Son of God!" they exclaimed.

34 After they had crossed the lake, they landed at Gennesaret. 35 When the people recognized Jesus, the news of his arrival spread quickly throughout the whole area, and soon people were bringing all their sick to be healed. 36 They begged him to let the sick touch at least the fringe of his robe, and all who touched him were healed."

Matthew 4: 22-36

Peter has always been one of my favorite disciples—he's just so human. Passionate, impulsive, and honest. He makes bold promises he can't keep, asks impossible questions, and wears his heart on his sleeve in ways that are both
inspiring and messy.

I often think about the moment Peter stepped out of the boat to walk toward Jesus on the water. Jesus said yes to Peter's wild request—and for a few steps, Peter actually walked on the waves. But then fear crept in. The wind howled. The water churned. And he began to sink. Jesus reached out to save him, saying, "O you of little faith."

When I was younger, I always heard those words as a rebuke. Peter had talked big, but when things got hard, he panicked. In my mind, Jesus' tone was sharp—disappointed.

But the older I get, and the more I live through my own sinking moments, the more I hear something else in His voice. Not condemnation, but compassion. Maybe even a touch of humor. Almost as if He's saying, "Oh Peter, you almost had it. You're learning. Come on, I've got you."

I've come to see myself in Peter—most of us can. We make promises to trust, to stay calm, to believe. And then life hits hard, and suddenly, we're gasping for air.

Many of us carry quiet shame for not being steadier, stronger, or more faithful.

But I don't think Jesus was surprised by Peter's fear any more than He's surprised by ours. He knows exactly how human we are—and He meets us there.

Too often, we live under the wrong kind of fear of God. Not the holy awe that draws us to worship, but the anxious fear that keeps us flinching, bracing for punishment. We mix up conviction with condemnation. But because of Jesus, we don't have to be afraid of God's presence. We can come to Him in our trembling and still find His hand reaching out to catch us.

He isn't waiting for perfection; He's inviting us to be fully human—with all our doubts, fears, and messiness—and to trust that His response will always be kindness, patience, and love.

1 Reading & Personal Reflection

Read the Scriptures and the devotional. Write down your first thoughts.

Ask yourself:
What part of this passage or reflection stands out most to me?

In what ways might you relate to Peter?

Is there a part of me resisting or longing to connect with God right now?

Jesus,
You invite me to step out of the safety of the boat,
to take a risk of faith,
even when the wind howls around me.

I tremble at the waves, at my own doubt,
at the fear that I will falter.

Yet You reach out Your hand,
steadying me when I stumble,
lifting me when I sink.

Teach me to trust Your presence,
to embrace my humanity—my boldness, my mistakes, my messiness—
and to step toward You, again and again,
knowing that Your love meets me in every falter.

Amen.

2

Contemplative Prayer

Sit quietly, breathe deeply, and read the prayer slowly. Pause to reflect, notice your thoughts and feelings, and rest in God's presence.

Deeper Reflection
Take a moment to dig deeper into these vereses and answer the questions below:

What does Peter's experience teach us about the relationship between faith and fear? Can doubt coexist with true faith?

How might Jesus' gentle response—"O ye of little faith"—reframe the way we understand God's patience with human frailty?

In what ways does stepping out in faith require vulnerability?

How can embracing our human imperfections deepen our trust in God rather than diminish it?

_____
_____
_____
_____
_____
_____
_____
_____
_____
_____
_____
_____
_____

Journal about a time you "stepped out of the boat"—took a risk in faith—and felt fear or doubt.

Write about how God met you in that moment.

Draw or visualize a scene of yourself walking on water toward Jesus, capturing the tension of fear and the reassurance of His hand.

Compose a short prayer, poem, or song reflecting both boldness and faltering faith.

4

Creative Practice

Create something that helps you meditate on the Scripture and devotional.

Community & Service

Identify someone who is hesitant or fearful about stepping out in faith or pursuing a challenging path. Offer encouragement, practical help, or simply your presence.

Consider sharing your story of doubt and trust with a friend, mentor, or small group, showing how God meets us in our human fragility.

Engage in a small act of courage or service that pushes you out of your comfort zone, trusting that God will guide and uphold you.

_____
_____
_____
_____
_____
_____
_____
_____
_____
_____
_____
_____

Sit quietly and reflect on Peter's moment on the water.

Breathe slowly, inhaling courage, exhaling fear.

Visualize Jesus' hand reaching for you, steadying you amid the waves of life.

Let yourself rest in the assurance that stepping out does not require perfection, only presence.

Feel the tension release as you entrust your doubts, your boldness, and your humanity to Him.

Rest in the truth: even when you falter, He is holding you.

6

Rest Practice

The Search for the Donkeys

" He is setting a table in the presence of our enemies. He is preparing a place right beside Him."

15 "Now the Lord had told Samuel the previous day,

16 "About this time tomorrow I will send you a man from the land of Benjamin. Anoint him to be the leader of my people, Israel. He will rescue them from the Philistines, for I have looked down on my people in mercy and have heard their cry."

17 When Samuel saw Saul, the Lord said, "That's the man I told you about! He will rule my people."

18 Just then Saul approached Samuel at the gateway and asked, "Can you please tell me where the seer's house is?" 19 "I am the seer!" Samuel replied. "Go up to the place of worship ahead of me. We will eat there together, and in the morning I'll tell you what you want to know and send you on your way.

20 And don't worry about those donkeys that were lost three days ago, for they have been found. And I am here to tell you that you and your family are the focus of all Israel's hopes."

21 Saul replied, "But I'm only from the tribe of Benjamin, the smallest tribe in Israel, and my family is the least important of all the families of that tribe! Why are you talking like this to me?"

22 Then Samuel brought Saul and his servant into the hall and placed them at the head of the table, honoring them above the thirty special guests. 23 Samuel then instructed the cook to bring Saul the finest cut of meat, the piece that had been set aside for the guest of honor. 24 So the cook brought in the meat and placed it before Saul. "Go ahead and eat it," Samuel said. "I was saving it for you even before I invited these others!" So Saul ate with Samuel that day. 25 When they came down from the place of worship and returned to town, Samuel took Saul up to the roof of the house and prepared a bed for him there. 26 At daybreak the next morning, Samuel called to Saul, "Get up! It's time you were on your way." So Saul got ready, and he and Samuel left the house together. 27 When they reached the edge of town, Samuel told Saul to send his servant on ahead. After the servant was gone, Samuel said, "Stay here, for I have received a special message for you from God."

1 Samuel 9:15–27

1 Samuel 9 tells us that on the day Saul was to be named king, his father sent him out to find their lost donkeys. Saul, in simple obedience, went. He traveled through the hill country of Ephraim, the land of Shalishah, the area of Shallim, and the entire land of Benjamin, which was roughly 40 to 60 miles.

At one point, Saul tells his servant, "Let's go back. My father is probably more worried about us than the donkeys." But the servant suddenly has this "random" thought that there is a man of God nearby who might be able to tell them where to go. Saul hesitates, mentioning that they have nothing to offer him, but the servant convinces him to go anyway.

At the same time, God had already told Samuel that He would reveal the man who would become Israel's leader. So Samuel begins traveling to the exact town where Saul is unknowingly headed. As soon as Samuel lays eyes on Saul, God draws his attention to him. Saul is still preoccupied with the missing donkeys, and Samuel tells him they have already been found and that Saul will be the focus of all Israel's hopes.
Saul immediately pushes back and says, "I am from the smallest tribe and my family is the least of all the families." Despite his hesitation, Samuel prepares a table for him, brings out the finest cut of meat, and makes this beautiful remark: "I was saving it for you even before I invited these others." It is a fascinating story. A few chapters later, trouble arises, and we find Saul coming in from the field behind the oxen. This is the anointed king of Israel, still working, still doing the everyday tasks.

Here is what caught my eye. When Samuel found Saul, Saul was simply going about his business and faithfully obeying his father. He was searching and searching for the donkeys. That very obedience led him straight to Samuel and straight into his calling without him even realizing it. If he had decided to do something else or take the day off, I wonder if Samuel would have found him at all.

Meanwhile, Samuel is preparing to change this young man's life. He is walking toward the exact town where Saul will be. He has already set aside the finest portion of meat, long before he even knows who Saul is. And although there was likely a waiting period between the anointing and the establishment of the kingdom, we still find Saul working the fields. He was living in the ordinary, practicing quiet obedience and dedication. Both donkey-searching and field-working are grounding tasks. Saul was simply doing the next right thing.

When we walk through suffering, it often feels like we have lost our grounding. The life we once knew feels gone, and we feel untethered. Saul's story is a reminder of what we can do while we wait for God to move on our behalf. We can be obedient to what He has already asked us to do. I will not pretend that it is easy or enjoyable, but tasks like Saul's can be incredibly grounding. They anchor us when everything else feels hard and uncertain.

And just as God did for Saul, He uses our obedience to move us in the right direction, which is toward Him. When we cannot even imagine where the donkeys are, He is preparing the finest cut of meat for us. He is
setting a table in the presence of our enemies. He is preparing a place right beside Him.

Beloved, be encouraged that in the midst of our ordinary and obedient lives, God is moving on our behalf with healing, restoration, and deliverance.

Reading & Personal Reflection

Read the Scriptures and the devotional. Write down your first thoughts.

Ask yourself:
What part of this passage or reflection stands out most to me?

Does it feel easy or hard to walk in obedience in the day to day tasks?

Is there a part of me resisting or longing to connect with God right now?

_____
_____
_____
_____
_____
_____
_____
_____
_____
_____
_____
_____
_____
_____

God of the unseen,
You move in ways we cannot always perceive,
guiding our steps even when they seem small or mundane.

As Saul walked to find donkeys, You were already orchestrating destiny.

Teach me to trust the ordinary tasks, the quiet obedience, the daily rhythms of life.

Open my eyes to Your presence in the everyday,
to Your hand working behind the scenes,
preparing a table I cannot yet see,
a plan that unfolds in Your perfect timing.

Help me surrender the need to control the path,
to rest in the truth that You are faithful,
that You are at work, even when I am unaware,
and that Your plans are greater than my understanding.

Amen.

2

Contemplative Prayer

Sit quietly, breathe deeply, and read the prayer slowly. Pause to reflect, notice your thoughts and feelings, and rest in God's presence.

Deeper Reflection
Take a moment to dig deeper into these vereses and answer the questions below:

How does Saul's story challenge our assumptions about what it means to be "chosen" by God?

In what ways does God work behind the scenes in our lives, even when we are unaware or focused on mundane tasks?

How might obedience in ordinary moments position us for extraordinary purposes?

How can recognizing God's "hidden work" change our perspective on the challenges or routines of daily life?

_____
_____
_____
_____
_____
_____
_____
_____
_____
_____
_____
_____
_____

Journal about a time when ordinary or routine tasks unexpectedly led to something meaningful in your life.

Draw or visualize a table being prepared for you, as a metaphor for God's unseen provision, waiting for the right time to reveal itself.

Consider a photo or sketch project capturing small, everyday moments that might be part of God's larger story—like a journey, a meal, or a simple act of service.

4

Creative Practice

Create something that helps you meditate on the Scripture and devotional.

Community & Service

Identify someone in your life whose work or obedience may seem ordinary or unseen, and encourage them, acknowledging God's work in their efforts.

Engage in an act of service—however small—trusting that God is using it for His purposes.

Pray specifically for awareness of God's orchestration in your own and others' everyday lives.

Sit quietly and breathe, reflecting on God's unseen work in your life.

Visualize each small step, each act of obedience, being part of a larger tapestry He is weaving.

Release your worry that your ordinary efforts are insignificant.

Breathe in trust, breathe out doubt.

Rest in the knowledge that, like Saul, your daily obedience positions you for God's timing, provision, and purposes.

Let your heart settle in the quiet assurance that He is preparing the table, even before you realize it.

6

Rest Practice

Mustard Seed Faith

"In our own lives, faith often comes the same way—through tiny, daily acts, practiced and sustained by the Spirit."

14 "At the foot of the mountain, a large crowd was waiting for them. A man came and knelt before Jesus and said, 15 "Lord, have mercy on my son. He has seizures and suffers terribly. He often falls into the fire or into the water. 16 So I brought him to your disciples, but they couldn't heal him. 17 Jesus said, "You faithless and corrupt people! How long must I be with you? How long must I put up with you? Bring the boy here to me." 18 Then Jesus rebuked the demon in the boy, and it left him. From that moment the boy was well. 19 Afterward the disciples asked Jesus privately, "Why couldn't we cast out that demon?" 20 "You don't have enough faith," Jesus told them. "I tell you the truth, if you had faith even as small as a mustard seed, you could say to this mountain, 'Move from here to there,' and it would move. Nothing would be impossible."

Matthew 17: 14-20

11 "Faith shows the reality of what we hope for; it is the evidence of things we cannot see. 2 Through their faith, the people in days of old earned a good reputation. 3 By faith we understand that the entire universe was formed at God's command, that what we now see did not come from anything that can be seen. 32 How much more do I need to say? It would take too long to recount the stories of the faith of Gideon, Barak, Samson, Jephthah, David, Samuel, and all the prophets. 33 By faith these people overthrew kingdoms, ruled with justice, and received what God had promised them. They shut the mouths of lions, 34 quenched the flames of fire, and escaped death by the edge of the sword. Their weakness was turned to strength. They became strong in battle and put whole armies to flight. 35 Women received their loved ones back again from death. 39 All these people earned a good reputation because of their faith, yet none of them received all that God had promised. 40 For God had something better in mind for us, so that they would not reach perfection without us."

Hebrews 11:1-3, 32-35, 39-40

12 'Therefore, since we are surrounded by such a huge crowd of witnesses to the life of faith, let us strip off every weight that slows us down, especially the sin that so easily trips us up. And let us run with endurance the race God has set before us. 2 We do this by keeping our eyes on Jesus, the champion who initiates and perfects our faith.[a] Because of the joy[b] awaiting him, he endured the cross, disregarding its shame. Now he is seated in the place of honor beside God's throne. 3 Think of all the hostility he endured from sinful people;[c] then you won't become weary and give up."

Hebrews 12: 1-3

For a long time, the image of "faith the size of a mustard seed" frustrated me. It felt dismissive—like a platitude offered to those barely hanging on. But I've come to see that Jesus wasn't minimizing faith; He was dignifying the smallest, most fragile kind of belief.

Most of us imagine faith as steady and radiant—full of courage and certainty. But faith rarely feels that way. It's quiet, often trembling, yet persistent. Sometimes it's nothing more than a whispered prayer or the choice to take one small step forward when everything in us wants to stop.

Mustard-seed faith is not flashy—it's stubborn. It refuses to let despair have the final word. It chooses to believe that God is still good, still present, even when every circumstance argues otherwise.

I think of Noah building the ark, day after day, with not a single rain cloud in sight. Or the Israelites in exile, waiting for God to call them back to the Promised Land. In both, there was likely a small spark that kept reaching for God, that kept showing up, trusting Him when nothing made sense.

In our own lives, faith often comes the same way—through tiny, daily acts, practiced and sustained by the Spirit. Our part is small—showing up when we can, praying when we remember, trusting when we feel fragile. But the Author of our faith does what only He can do: He waters the seed, softens the heart, and grows something new from even the smallest spark.

It turns out that's all He ever asked for—a mustard seed of faith. He shows us that the smallest, most fragile choice to trust Him can change everything.

Reading & Personal Reflection

Read the Scriptures and the devotional. Write down your first thoughts.

Ask yourself:
What part of this passage or reflection stands out most to me?

In what areas of my life do I have a mustard seed of faith?

Is there a part of me resisting or longing to connect with God right now?

_____

_____

_____

_____

_____

_____

_____

_____

_____

_____

_____

_____

_____

Jesus,
You call me to faith, even when it feels small,
fragile, or trembling.

I confess that sometimes I have measured faith by
my feelings— by courage I do not feel, peace I
cannot grasp, trust I cannot sustain.

Yet You remind me that even the tiniest seed of faith,
held in Your hand, is enough.

Water it, Lord.
Nurture it. Make it grow.

Teach me to show up, even half-heartedly, and trust
that You are at work in ways I cannot see.

Let me rest in the quiet power of Your sustaining love,
knowing that my small, trembling faith is never too
little for You.

Amen.

Contemplative Prayer

Sit quietly, breathe deeply, and read the prayer slowly. Pause to reflect, notice your thoughts and feelings, and rest in God's presence.

Deeper Reflection
Take a moment to dig deeper into these vereses and answer the questions below:

What does it mean that faith is a choice rather than a feeling? How does this change the way we approach our spiritual lives?

How does God's role as the "Author of faith" shape our understanding of human effort and divine action?

How can small acts of faith—showing up to Bible study, prayer, worship—be meaningful, even when our hearts feel dry or doubtful?

How does this perspective shift the way you respond to your own spiritual doubts or seasons of dryness?

_____
_____
_____
_____
_____
_____
_____
_____
_____
_____
_____
_____

Journal about a "mustard seed moment" in your life—when you took a small step of faith and God nurtured it.

Write a short prayer or poem celebrating the hidden growth that occurs when we simply show up, even imperfectly.

Draw or sketch a mustard seed and surrounding imagery, representing the growth that God brings from small beginnings.

4

Creative Practice

Create something that helps you meditate on the Scripture and devotional.

Community & Service

Encourage someone who feels their faith is too small or weak, sharing the reminder that God can nurture even the tiniest mustard seed.

Offer to pray with someone quietly, focusing on small, faithful steps rather than grand gestures.

Serve in a small, consistent way—helping a neighbor, volunteering, or offering support—trusting that God can use these ordinary acts to grow something greater.

_____
_____
_____
_____
_____
_____
_____
_____
_____
_____
_____
_____
_____

Sit quietly and breathe, imagining your mustard seed of faith resting in God's hand.

As you inhale, picture God nurturing and watering it.

As you exhale, release pressure, worry, or the need to "feel" faith fully.

Sit in the stillness, trusting that God is at work, growing something new and unseen.

Visualize your small step of faith—showing up, praying, singing, reading Scripture—being transformed into life and growth by His care.

Rest in the truth: even the tiniest seed, held by the Author of faith, is enough.

6
Rest Practice

The God Who Moves First

"He has cleared the path, shortened the distance, and made a way for us to always run into the Father's arms."

"

1 "Once you were dead because of your disobedience and your many sins. 2 You used to live in sin, just like the rest of the world, obeying the devil—the commander of the powers in the unseen world.[a] He is the spirit at work in the hearts of those who refuse to obey God. 3 All of us used to live that way, following the passionate desires and inclinations of our sinful nature. By our very nature we were subject to God's anger, just like everyone else. 4 But God is so rich in mercy, and he loved us so much, 5 that even though we were dead because of our sins, he gave us life when he raised Christ from the dead. (It is only by God's grace that you have been saved!) 6 For he raised us from the dead along with Christ and seated us with him in the heavenly realms because we are united with Christ Jesus. 7 So God can point to us in all future ages as examples of the incredible wealth of his grace and kindness toward us, as shown in all he has done for us who are united with Christ Jesus. 8 God saved you by his grace when you believed. And you can't take credit for this; it is a gift from God. 9 Salvation is not a reward for the good things we have done, so none of us can boast about it. 10 For we are God's masterpiece. He has created us anew in Christ Jesus, so we can do the good things he planned for us long ago."

Ephesians 2:1-10

Believe it or not—God is obsessed with you. Not in a distant, abstract way, but with a love so fierce, so consuming, that He sent His Son to die so that you could spend eternity with Him.

Ephesians 2:1–3 reminds us of where this love began to find us: "As for you, you were dead in your transgressions and sins, in which you used to live when you followed the ways of this world... All of us also lived among them at one time, gratifying the cravings of our flesh and following its desires and thoughts. Like the rest, we were by nature deserving of wrath."

Let's pause here—what are dead things capable of? Can they grow, move, or choose something different? Of course not. And yet, how often do we act as though we were the ones who chose God first—as though He were standing off to the side waiting for us to finally come to our senses?

The truth is far more beautiful: before we ever turned toward Him, He moved first. Before we had the strength to choose Him, He chose us. Before we could even recognize our sin, He saw us—and still came running. As people dead in sin, we were powerless to reach for life. But God, in His kindness, awakened us. He breathed life into what was lifeless and empowered us to respond. Even our ability to choose Him is a miracle of His mercy. After we accept Him, we remain utterly dependent on His Spirit to make us holy. We cannot sanctify ourselves any more than we could save ourselves.

So what does He do? He clothes us in the righteousness of Christ and calls it finished. And then, in His gentleness, He walks with us day by day, shaping us, steadying us, teaching us how to live in the freedom He's already secured. We know sin still knocks at the door, and even our moments of obedience are carried by His Spirit. And one day, when we finally stand before Him, He will open the Book of Life and find our names—not because of what we've done, but because of what Christ has done for us.

That's how obsessed He is—with you, with me, with us. He didn't just make a way—He is the way, from beginning to end. Every step toward Him has already been paved by His grace. Sometimes we get so caught up in doing and striving—trying to live right, look right, be right—that we forget He's been doing the heavy lifting all along.

It reminds me of a child learning to walk. At first, a parent steadies them by the hands. Then, when the child begins to wobble forward, the parent moves obstacles out of the way, cheering every step. And when the child stumbles, the parent moves closer—closing the gap—until the child can reach them.

That's exactly what Christ has done for us. He has cleared the path, shortened the distance, and made a way for us to always run into the Father's arms. God doesn't always cause our suffering, but He never wastes it. He is always near it. Scripture tells us, "He is close to the brokenhearted and saves those who are crushed in spirit." (Psalm 34:18) He is the Father who refuses to leave. The One who keeps moving toward us, even when we can't move toward Him. The One who made sure that from beginning to end—from death to life, from wandering to home—we would never, ever be alone.

Reading & Personal Reflection

Read the Scriptures and the devotional. Write down your first thoughts.

Ask yourself:
What part of this passage or reflection stands out most to me?

How does it move my heart to know that God started the pursuit for me?

Is there a part of me resisting or longing to connect with God right now?

_____
_____
_____
_____
_____
_____
_____
_____
_____
_____
_____
_____
_____

*O God, who moved first,
You loved me before I could even respond.
You breathed life into what was lifeless,
ran toward me when I was
wandering, and called me Your own before
I had words to say.*

*Teach me to rest in that grace,
to trust that I am already held, already known,
already loved.*

*When I stumble, steady my steps.
When I grieve, bend low to lift me.*

*When I doubt, remind me that even now, You
are moving toward me, from death to life, from
fear to freedom, from wandering to home.*

Amen.

2

Contemplative Prayer

Sit quietly, breathe deeply, and read the prayer slowly. Pause to reflect, notice your thoughts and feelings, and rest in God's presence.

Deeper Reflection
Take a moment to dig deeper into these vereses and answer the questions below:

How does understanding that God initiated His love for us change the way we approach faith and obedience?

In what ways is our sanctification a continuation of God's initial act of love and resurrection?

How might viewing life as a journey from death to life, guided by God's pursuit, shape the way we interpret our hardships, relationships, and growth?

Journal about a moment when you felt God moving first in your life—before you could seek Him or understand His plan.

Write a short poem, song, or prayer imagining God pursuing you in the places you feel dead, broken, or unseen.

Create a visual representation of God's presence in your life, focusing on His active pursuit and care—like hands reaching out, light breaking through darkness, or paths being prepared.

4

Creative Practice

Create something that helps you meditate on the Scripture and devotional.

Community & Service

Walk around your neighborhood, workplace, or local park and silently pray for the people you pass.

Choose someone in your life or community who doesn't yet follow Christ. Commit to praying daily for God to move first in their heart, providing guidance, protection, and opportunities to encounter His love.

Invite a neighbor, co-worker, or friend who isn't yet part of a faith community to a simple meal, coffee, or community event—an opportunity to build a relationship without pressure, showing God's love through hospitality.

_____
_____
_____
_____
_____
_____
_____
_____
_____
_____
_____
_____

Sit quietly and breathe deeply.

Imagine God's hand reaching for you, moving toward you, calling you alive.

As you inhale, sense His presence surrounding you.
As you exhale, release the need to perform, fix, or understand everything.

Visualize yourself resting in His grace, fully alive, fully loved, fully known.

Let your heart settle in the truth: God moved first, and He continues to move toward you—even here, even now.

Remain in that quiet assurance for 5–10 minutes, letting your soul be renewed by His unwavering love.

6
Rest Practice

Wrestling with God

"You aren't going to win this one, but if you are bold enough to wrestle with Him, You are going to get something better than answers."

> 24 "Then Jacob was left alone, and a man wrestled with him until daybreak. 25 When the man saw that he could not overpower him, he touched the socket of Jacob's hip so that his hip was wrenched as he wrestled with the man. 26 Then the man said, 'Let me go, for it is daybreak.' But Jacob replied, 'I will not let you go unless you bless me.' The man asked him, 27 'What is your name?' 'Jacob,' he answered. Then the man said, 28 'Your name will no longer be Jacob, but Israel, because you have struggled with God and with humans and have overcome.'"

Genesis 32:24–28

During one of my more recent seasons of suffering, I often felt like Jacob wrestling with the angel. I wasn't necessarily asking for God's blessing—at least not at first. I was wrestling with His goodness, pleading for any kind of relief, any glimmer of understanding. So maybe I was asking for His blessing after all. But what I found was something deeper. If we look at the context of Jacob's wrestling match, we find him between two threats: behind him, Laban; ahead of him, Esau, who had every reason to despise him. In Genesis 32, Jacob prays for God to keep His promise to his ancestors—that his descendants would be "too numerous to count."

He then sends everyone over and finds himself alone with the man. Scripture tells us that Jacob wrestled through the night with a man, refusing to let go until he received a blessing. The text later reveals what Jacob must have already known: this was no ordinary man. "I have seen God face to face," he says, "and yet my life has been spared." You don't ask for blessings from strangers. Jacob wrestled with God Himself—clinging, fighting, refusing to let go until he could be sure that the same God who blessed Abraham and Isaac would also be his God.

One commentary states, "The significance of the passage lies primarily in Jacob's discovering the freedom and enduring grace of God. The passage shows that God is free to bless whom he pleases. The blessing Jacob so desires is not an automatic bestowal based on God's promises to his fathers, Abraham and Isaac. Nor is it a promise Jacob can achieve through his own strength or wit."
I wonder if there was a part of Jacob that needed to know for himself that God was who He said He was. It's one thing to hear the stories of God's faithfulness to others—it's another to encounter Him in the dark night of your own fear. I imagine Jacob's desperate cry: "Help me. Show me. Bless me." And that act of wrestling was itself an act of faith.

Now don't forget, He didn't emerge from this wrestle unscathed. The angel touched his hip, and he walked with a limp. His limp would be the beautiful reminder that He saw God, that He could wrestle with Him, and He could be bold enough to ask Him to show up for him. It was a reminder that God is able and will for his people.

I walk with a limp these days. I actually have more questions than answers. I know less about life than I knew before. And yet, I know God more intimately. I have come to know Him more as a caring and present Father rather than a far off God, just watching to see how my life plays out. God has encouraged and built up my faith, and I like Jacob feel a lot bolder to ask of God - not just in the material things, that He would be closer to me and that He would let me know Him more, and that I would love Him more.

Beloved, He offers the same invitation to you in your suffering. He is not afraid of your questions. He is not offended by your wrestling. He welcomes it. He is safe to wrestle with. He will even let you think you are
winning, not to taunt you, but to invite you deeper. He wants you to get up close to him, to look him straight in the eyes, and to ask him the very hard and heavy questions. He desires for you to ask Him to show up for you, and wants you to call Him on His promises. Contrary to popular opinion, this is not a sign of doubt but actually an act of bold faith. It's saying, "I don't understand, but I believe You can meet me here."

You may walk away with a limp. You aren't going to win this one, but if you are bold enough to wrestle with Him, You are going to get something better than answers. You will leave changed and marked, because you too have seen the face of God and lived.

Reading & Personal Reflection

Read the Scriptures and the devotional. Write down your first thoughts.

Ask yourself:
What part of this passage or reflection stands out most to me?

How do I feel about wrestling with God? And what am I wrestling with God about?

Is there a part of me resisting or longing to connect with God right now?

_____
_____
_____
_____
_____
_____
_____
_____
_____
_____
_____
_____
_____
_____

God of the night wrestles,

*You meet me not in comfort but in struggle,
not in certainty but in the trembling of my heart.*

*You let me cling to You in the darkness—
breathing, fighting, pleading, refusing to let go until
You bless me.*

*I am not who I was before I met You here.
My faith limps, but it walks.*

*My questions linger, but so does Your presence.
Teach me not to fear the wrestle — to find You
in the ache, to trust that Your nearness is the
blessing.*

Amen.

2

Contemplative Prayer

Sit quietly, breathe deeply, and read the prayer slowly. Pause to reflect, notice your thoughts and feelings, and rest in God's presence.

3 Deeper Reflection

Take a moment to dig deeper into these vereses and answer the questions below:

What does Jacob's wrestling reveal about the kind of relationship God desires with His people?

How can our struggles and doubts become acts of faith rather than signs of failure?

What do you think it means to be "marked" by God—physically, emotionally, or spiritually—after encountering Him?

How do we reconcile a God who both wounds and blesses?

_____
_____
_____
_____
_____
_____
_____
_____
_____
_____
_____
_____
_____
_____

Write a journal entry or poem from Jacob's perspective after the encounter—what might he have said, limping away in dawn's first light?

Sketch or paint what "wrestling with God" looks like to you. Is it a struggle, an embrace, or both?

Create a playlist of songs that mirror your own wrestling with faith—songs that hold both ache and hope.

Write a letter to God beginning with, "This is what I don't understand..." and let it unfold honestly.

4 *Creative Practice*

Create something that helps you meditate on the Scripture and devotional.

Community & Service

Pray with someone who's struggling. Instead of giving answers, simply sit with them—wrestle alongside them.

Engage in an act of presence this week: listen to a friend's story without trying to fix it. Practice the ministry of "being with."

Consider writing a note of encouragement to someone who has shown you what faithful wrestling looks like.

_____
_____
_____
_____
_____
_____
_____
_____
_____
_____
_____
_____
_____

Find a quiet place and settle your body.
Close your eyes and imagine Jacob at daybreak—limping, but alive.
Feel your own "limp"—the tender, imperfect places in you that
have come from wrestling.

Place a hand over your heart and breathe deeply.

Inhale: You are near.
Exhale: I am still Yours.

Let yourself rest in that paradox: that wrestling and resting are not
opposites, that God meets you not despite the struggle but in it.

Linger in silence, knowing He calls you beloved,
even here—especially here.

6

Rest Practice

Refined by Fire

"He's not trying to destroy you. He's drawing near. The flames are not proof of His absence."

"In this you greatly rejoice, even though now for a little while, if necessary, you have been distressed by various trials, so that the proof of your faith, being more precious than gold which is perishable, even though tested by fire, may be found to result in praise and glory and honor at the revelation of Jesus Christ; and though you have not seen Him, you love Him, and though you do not see Him now, but believe in Him, you greatly rejoice with joy inexpressible and full of glory."

1 Peter 1:6–7

"Each man's work will become evident; for the day will disclose it, because it will be revealed with fire, and the fire itself will test the quality of each man's work."

1 Corinthians 3:13

Throughout Scripture, fire represents the presence of God. It's how He revealed Himself to Moses in the burning bush, how He led Israel through the wilderness, and how His Spirit fell at Pentecost. In the temple, a special fire burned continuously, started by God Himself.

Deuteronomy says God is a consuming fire, a jealous God. Fire marks His nearness—
His holiness that purifies, His power that cannot be contained.

But fire also refines and reveals. Fire burns away what cannot last. It tests what is real.
If I'm honest, I've often prayed for God's presence without realizing that sometimes
His presence comes as refining flames. God wants to reveal what we are truly made
of—stripping away creature comforts, defenses, and maladaptive coping mechanisms.
Suffering, although uncomfortable and sometimes painful, reveals our true nature and places us in a posture of humility before Him.

This process is not pretty—but what if the heat is actually evidence that He's closer than we thought? Like a refiner at the furnace, the Father never leaves the metal unattended. If silver is left too long in the fire, it loses its value. God watches carefully, knowing exactly how much heat we can bear and exactly how long it takes to reveal what is pure.

He's not trying to destroy you. He's drawing near. The flames are not proof of His absence—they are proof of His hand. When the fire feels too hot, remember: the refiner stays close. His eyes are on you. His presence fills even the places that burn. Don't mistake the fire for abandonment. It may be the most tangible sign that the Father is near—refining, shaping, and revealing His image in you.

Reading & Personal Reflection

Read the Scriptures and the devotional. Write down your first thoughts.

Ask yourself:
What part of this passage or reflection stands out most to me?

Are there places in my life where God is refining me?

Is there a part of me resisting or longing to connect with God right now?

_____
_____
_____
_____
_____
_____
_____
_____
_____
_____
_____
_____

*Refining God,
You are fire that does not consume,
yet burns away what is false.*

You come close in the flames, in the heat, in the moments that test me most.

*Teach me to recognize Your presence even
in suffering, to see Your refining hand in every trial.*

*When I feel scorched, remind me that You are not
absent, but drawing near—shaping, purifying,
and revealing what is truly Yours in me.*

*Hold me steady in the furnace, O Lord,
and let Your Spirit ignite courage, hope,
and unwavering faith.*

Amen.

2

Contemplative Prayer

*Sit quietly, breathe deeply, and read the prayer slowly. Pause to reflect,
notice your thoughts and feelings, and rest in God's presence.*

Deeper Reflection
Take a moment to dig deeper into these vereses and answer the questions below:

How can trials be understood as evidence of God's closeness rather than His absence?

In what ways can recognizing the refining fire transform our understanding of prayer, obedience, and spiritual growth?

How does God's careful attention during the refining process reflect His intimate knowledge of and care for us?

Journal about a time when you felt tested or burned by life's circumstances—how did God reveal Himself in that fire?

Write a metaphorical reflection or poem about being refined, purged, or purified by the Father's fire.

Sketch or visualize the process of refining—perhaps a furnace, metal, and a careful, watchful hand shaping what is pure.

4

Creative Practice

Create something that helps you meditate on the Scripture and devotional.

Community & Service

Create a physical or digital space (bulletin board, shared doc, or social media group) where people can anonymously post "lessons learned from refining" or moments of growth through trials. Read through and pray over the shared experiences.

Volunteer or serve in ways that require patience or persistence, recognizing that God often works through perseverance.

Reflect on the ways your own refined character can encourage or serve others who are being shaped by trials.

_____
_____
_____
_____
_____
_____
_____
_____
_____
_____
_____
_____
_____
_____
_____

Find a quiet space and breathe slowly.
Picture a piece of silver or gold in the hands of a careful refiner.

Imagine God's watchful eyes, His presence in the heat, and the flames purifying and revealing the essence of what is real and true.

As you inhale, sense His nearness and attention.

As you exhale, release fear, frustration, or the desire to rush the process.

Rest in the knowledge that the fire is not abandonment—it is intimacy, refinement, and love.

Let your soul linger in the truth: even in the heat, God is near, shaping and revealing His image in you.

6
Rest Practice

Highly Esteemed

"But make no mistake—God moves when His people pray."

>

"While I was still speaking in prayer, the man Gabriel, whom I had seen in the vision previously, came to me in my extreme weariness about the time of the evening offering. He gave me instruction and talked with me and said, 'O Daniel, I have now come forth to give you insight with understanding. At the beginning of your supplications, the command was issued, and I have come to tell you, for you are highly esteemed; so give heed to the message and gain understanding of the vision.'"

Daniel 9:20–23

"The Lord is close to the brokenhearted and saves those who are crushed in spirit."

Psalm 34:18

During seasons of suffering, it can be really easy for us to believe that God isn't moving on our behalf- especially when things aren't changing. Things aren't getting better in your marriage. Your kiddos are still making the same decisions, and despite the multiple rounds of chemo, the cancer remains. When Ruth, my mother-in-law, got sick, despite all the prayers, she didn't get better. She passed away in March after about 5 months of wrestling with COVID. Looking back now, I can see God's hand of mercy and grace on her life by taking her home. (Honestly, she was very ready to be with Jesus. She loved him with her whole heart.) But in that moment, it felt like betrayal.

Many of you, too, have experienced something similar - really important prayers gone in what feels like unanswered. And honestly, it's hard - it's a lonely place to be.
And please don't tell me, 'Prayer might not change the situation, but it changes you.' Can I be a real human right now? I hate that. (I do believe that to be true, but in suffering, I am not looking to be changed particularly as much as I am looking for a solution to my suffering.)

Then the other day, I found this little treasure tucked away in Daniel 9. Daniel is confessing and praying for the people of Israel after God had given He saw God's Word come to pass against the people of Israel. And the next few verses take my breath away. Daniel says, "While I was still speaking in prayer, then the man Gabriel, whom I had seen in the vision previously, came to me in my extreme weariness about the time of the evening offering. He gave me instruction and talked with me and said, 'O Daniel, I have now come forth to give you insight with understanding. At the beginning of your supplications, the command was issued, and I have come to tell you, for you are highly esteemed; so give heed to the message and gain understanding of the vision'."

God sent Gabriel before he even finished praying and met him in his words, "my extreme weariness." Gabriel makes it clear that the moment Daniel started praying, an answer was issued, because Daniel is highly esteemed. Highly esteemed by whom? God of the Universe. God, in his mercy, literally met Daniel exactly where he was - in his weariness, because God loved him and considered him so precious.

Gabriel meeting Daniel wasn't a traditional answer to his prayer. In fact, Gabriel provides two things: understanding and presence. Gabriel makes it clear that the answer to Daniel's prayer was the coming Messiah... the Messiah wouldn't make it to earth for another about 450 years. The answered prayer was still in motion. Daniel would have been watching his answered prayer from Heaven. Instead, God gives Daniel presence and an understanding of the hope to come.

Beloved, prayer does indeed change things—because prayer is communion with a God who listens, responds, and draws near. Sometimes the change looks like healing or reconciliation. Other times, it looks like endurance, mercy, or peace in the storm. And sometimes, like with Ruth, it looks like God's tender hand leading a beloved one home.

But make no mistake—God moves when His people pray. Because your prayers are heard, you too are highly esteemed by Him. The command has already been issued. The same God who met Daniel in his exhaustion is meeting you in yours.

Reading & Personal Reflection

Read the Scriptures and the devotional. Write down your first thoughts.

Ask yourself:
What part of this passage or reflection stands out most to me?

Do I consider myself highly esteemed by God?

Is there a part of me resisting or longing to connect with God right now?

_____

_____

_____

_____

_____

_____

_____

_____

_____

_____

_____

_____

_____

_____

God of the weary, You see me in my exhaustion, my frustration, my longing for relief.

When my prayers feel heavy or unanswered, You are still listening, still moving, still present in ways I cannot yet perceive.

Meet me here, Lord — in the waiting, in the questions, in the grief.

Teach me to rest in the truth that my words are not lost, that my prayers have already been heard, that I am highly esteemed by You, even when the answers seem delayed.

Amen.

Contemplative Prayer

Sit quietly, breathe deeply, and read the prayer slowly. Pause to reflect, notice your thoughts and feelings, and rest in God's presence.

Deeper Reflection
Take a moment to dig deeper into these vereses and answer the questions below:

What does Daniel's example teach us about God's timing versus our expectations?

How can we understand "answered prayer" when the response is presence or understanding rather than immediate change?

What does it mean to be "highly esteemed" by God, and how might that truth sustain us in suffering?

In what ways can endurance, mercy, and peace be considered answers to prayer?

_____
_____
_____
_____
_____
_____
_____
_____
_____
_____
_____

Journal about a prayer that feels unanswered and explore the ways God may have already been responding through presence, understanding, or hope.

Write a letter to God expressing your weariness and longing for change—then pause to imagine His response, like Gabriel's visit to Daniel.

Draw or paint your weariness as a landscape—then add symbols of God meeting you there.

Compose a poem or short prayer of hope rooted in God's unseen work, reminding yourself that His timing is perfect and His love is steadfast.

4

Creative Practice

Create something that helps you meditate on the Scripture and devotional.

Community & Service

Share your current struggles with a trusted friend or family member and pray for one another.

Offer to pray with someone in a space of weariness or grief, focusing on God's nearness rather than the solution.

Send notes, texts, or small gifts to people in your community who are also exhausted or grieving.

_____
_____
_____
_____
_____
_____
_____
_____
_____
_____
_____
_____
_____
_____

Find a quiet space and sit comfortably.

Close your eyes.

Visualize Daniel, weary and heavy-laden, speaking his prayers aloud.

Picture Gabriel appearing—not with immediate solutions, but with understanding and presence.

As you inhale, sense God's nearness and His listening heart.

As you exhale, release the need for immediate answers or change. Rest in the reality that your prayers are heard, that God is attentive, and that He is issuing answers even now.

Let your soul settle into peace, endurance, and hope—trusting that He is at work, even when you cannot yet see it.

6

Rest Practice

Our Daily Bread

"Our pain can make us blind. But when we open our eyes, we begin to notice His small (and big) provisions: a simple gift, a comforting Scripture, and supernatural joy."

"When you pray, don't be like the hypocrites who love to pray publicly on street corners and in the synagogues where everyone can see them. I tell you the truth, that is all the reward they will ever get. 6 But when you pray, go away by yourself, shut the door behind you, and pray to your Father in private. Then your Father, who sees everything, will reward you. 7 "When you pray, don't babble on and on as the Gentiles do. They think their prayers are answered merely by repeating their words again and again. 8 Don't be like them, for your Father knows exactly what you need even before you ask him! 9 Pray like this: Our Father in heaven, may your name be kept holy. 10 May your Kingdom come soon. May your will be done on earth, as it is in heaven. 11 Give us today the food we need, 12 and forgive us our sins, as we have forgiven those who sin against us. 13 And don't let us yield to temptation, but rescue us from the evil one. 14 "If you forgive those who sin against you, your heavenly Father will forgive you. 15 But if you refuse to forgive others, your Father will not forgive your sins."

Matthew 6:5-15

"Then the whole community of Israel set out from Elim and journeyed into the wilderness of Sin,[a] between Elim and Mount Sinai. They arrived there on the fifteenth day of the second month, one month after leaving the land of Egypt. 2 There, too, the whole community of Israel complained about Moses and Aaron. 3 "If only the Lord had killed us back in Egypt," they moaned. "There we sat around pots filled with meat and ate all the bread we wanted. But now you have brought us into this wilderness to starve us all to death." 4 Then the Lord said to Moses, "Look, I'm going to rain down food from heaven for you. Each day the people can go out and pick up as much food as they need for that day. I will test them in this to see whether or not they will follow my instructions. 5 On the sixth day they will gather food, and when they prepare it, there will be twice as much as usual." 6 So Moses and Aaron said to all the people of Israel, "By evening you will realize it was the Lord who brought you out of the land of Egypt. 7 In the morning you will see the glory of the Lord, because he has heard your complaints, which are against him, not against us. What have we done that you should complain about us?" 8 Then Moses added, "The Lord will give you meat to eat in the evening and bread to satisfy you in the morning, for he has heard all your complaints against him. What have we done? Yes, your complaints are against the Lord, not against us." 17 So the people of Israel did as they were told. Some gathered a lot, some only a little. 18 But when they measured it out, everyone had just enough. Those who gathered a lot had nothing left over, and those who gathered only a little had enough. Each family had just what it needed."

Exodus 16:1-8, 17-18

"Tomorrow has enough worries," and God seems to remind us of this every time He provides for His people. When He led Israel into the desert, He sent manna from heaven. He told them to gather enough for each day. If they tried to collect more than they needed, it would rot and fill with maggots. Yet, everyone—those who gathered a little and those who gathered a lot—had exactly what they needed for that day.

Jesus echoes this same truth in the Gospels, pointing us to the birds of the air and the lilies of the field. They neither toil nor spin, yet they are fed and clothed in glory. And then tell tells us plainly: do not worry about tomorrow.

In seasons of suffering, we can be tempted to rush toward the end, to hoard comforts, or overindulge, hoping to ease our pain. But when God leads us into our own deserts, times of wandering, uncertainty, and waiting, He invites us to trust Him. To learn to be sustained by Him, day by day. He, in His goodness and kindness, provides exactly what you need for the day ahead of you.

Our pain can make us blind. But when we open our eyes, we begin to notice His small (and big) provisions: a simple gift, a comforting Scripture, and supernatural joy.

Just like the Israelites, God gives us neither too much nor too little—just enough for today. And God asks us to trust that tomorrow, He will provide again—exactly what we need, exactly when we need it.

1 Reading & Personal Reflection

Read the Scriptures and the devotional. Write down your first thoughts.

Ask yourself:
What part of this passage or reflection stands out most to me?

Are there certain places in my life where I can see where God is providing me with my daily bread?

Is there a part of me resisting or longing to connect with God right now?

_____

_____

_____

_____

_____

_____

_____

_____

_____

_____

_____

_____

_____

_____

God of sustenance,
You give us exactly what we need, not too much,
not too little.

In the deserts of my life, teach me to trust Your
provision day by day.

Open my eyes to notice Your care in small ways:
the words that comfort, the meals that nourish, the
presence that steadies me.

Help me release my hoarding, my rushing, my
anxious grasping.

Remind me that You hold tomorrow in Your hands,
and that today, I have enough.

Amen.

2

Contemplative Prayer

Sit quietly, breathe deeply, and read the prayer slowly. Pause to reflect, notice your thoughts and feelings, and rest in God's presence.

Deeper Reflection
Take a moment to dig deeper into these vereses and answer the questions below:

How does God's provision of manna teach us to trust His timing and sufficiency?

In what ways do we "hoard" or overextend in our own lives instead of trusting daily provision?

How does recognizing God's daily care shift our perspective on suffering or scarcity?

How can daily reliance on God's provision deepen our relationship with Him and others?

_____
_____
_____
_____
_____
_____
_____
_____
_____
_____
_____
_____
_____

Write a poem or reflection imagining manna falling from heaven in your life—what does it look like, feel like, taste like?

Sketch or illustrate what "daily bread" looks like in your current season—physical, emotional, or spiritual.

Make a list of small blessings or moments of provision you might normally overlook, and meditate on them as sacred.

4

Creative Practice

Create something that helps you meditate on the Scripture and devotional.

Community & Service

Share a meal or provide for someone in need, focusing on small, tangible acts of care as God provides daily for them.

Volunteer in a setting that serves daily needs—food banks, shelters, or community kitchens—and reflect on God's provision in action.

Write a note or send a message to someone acknowledging a way God has met their daily needs recently.

Find a quiet space and sit comfortably.

Close your eyes and breathe slowly, imagining manna falling gently, enough for this day alone.

As you inhale, trust that God is providing.

As you exhale, release worry about tomorrow, unmet needs, or scarcity.

Let your soul rest in the rhythm of His daily care.

Know that God's provision is sufficient, and that each day He will give exactly what you need—bread for the body, nourishment for the soul, presence for the heart, when you cannot yet see it.

6
Rest Practice

Consider It Joy

"Joy is not a magic switch. It is an intentional practice, a posture of the heart, a choice to hold on to hope and beauty even when it's hard."

>

2 "Dear brothers and sisters,[a] when troubles of any kind come your way, consider it an opportunity for great joy. 3 For you know that when your faith is tested, your endurance has a chance to grow. 4 So let it grow, for when your endurance is fully developed, you will be perfect and complete, needing nothing. 5 If you need wisdom, ask our generous God, and he will give it to you. He will not rebuke you for asking. 6 But when you ask him, be sure that your faith is in God alone. Do not waver, for a person with divided loyalty is as unsettled as a wave of the sea that is blown and tossed by the wind. 7 Such people should not expect to receive anything from the Lord. 8 Their loyalty is divided between God and the world, and they are unstable in everything they do. 9 Believers who are[b] poor have something to boast about, for God has honored them. 10 And those who are rich should boast that God has humbled them. They will fade away like a little flower in the field. 11 The hot sun rises and the grass withers; the little flower droops and falls, and its beauty fades away. In the same way, the rich will fade away with all of their achievements. 12 God blesses those who patiently endure testing and temptation. Afterward they will receive the crown of life that God has promised to those who love him. 13 And remember, when you are being tempted, do not say, "God is tempting me." God is never tempted to do wrong,[c] and he never tempts anyone else. 14 Temptation comes from our own desires, which entice us and drag us away. 15 These desires give birth to sinful actions. And when sin is allowed to grow, it gives birth to death. 16 So don't be misled, my dear brothers and sisters. 17 Whatever is good and perfect is a gift coming down to us from God our Father, who created all the lights in the heavens.[d] He never changes or casts a shifting shadow.[e] 18 He chose to give birth to us by giving us his true word. And we, out of all creation, became his prized possession."

James 1:2–18

"Keep me safe, O God,
   for I have come to you for refuge.
2 I said to the Lord, "You are my Master!
   Every good thing I have comes from you."
3 The godly people in the land
   are my true heroes!
   I take pleasure in them!
4 Troubles multiply for those who chase after other gods.
   I will not take part in their sacrifices of blood
   or even speak the names of their gods.
5 Lord, you alone are my inheritance, my cup of blessing.
   You guard all that is mine.
6 The land you have given me is a pleasant land.
   What a wonderful inheritance!
7 I will bless the Lord who guides me;
   even at night my heart instructs me.
8 I know the Lord is always with me.
   I will not be shaken, for he is right beside me.
9 No wonder my heart is glad, and I rejoice.[b]
   My body rests in safety.
10 For you will not leave my soul among the dead[c]
   or allow your holy one[d] to rot in the grave.
11 You will show me the way of life,
   granting me the joy of your presence
   and the pleasures of living with you forever."

Psalm 16

When the world shut down in 2020, life felt heavy and uncertain. My husband and I were working from home, and our friend had lost her job while her husband still had to go into the office. Almost every day, our friend and her dog would come over. Together, we worked, laughed, ate, and napped.

Those moments of connection weren't easy. Some days were exhausting, frustrating, and even painful. Joy didn't just appear; we had to make room for it, sometimes against the weight of fear, grief, and uncertainty. Laughing, cooking, creating art, going for walks—it wasn't about pretending everything was fine. It was about holding on to life, to hope, to one another, in the midst of chaos.

James tells us to "consider it pure joy" in trials—not because the trial itself is good, but because God is present in it and working to grow you. God works even in our fear, our heartbreak, our uncertainty. Choosing joy doesn't erase pain or make the hard days easier. But it plants a seed of hope, a reminder that life, love, and God's presence cannot be destroyed by circumstance.

Some days, joy may feel impossible. Some days, you may only notice a tiny flicker of life: a text from a friend, a warm cup of coffee, a glimpse of sky through your window.
These moments may feel small, but they are rebellion against despair. They are reminders that even when life is messy, chaotic, or painful, God is still near.

Joy is not a magic switch. It is an intentional practice, a posture of the heart, a choice to hold on to hope and beauty even when it's hard. And in that choice, even the smallest flickers of delight become a tether—to life, to one another, and to the God who never abandons us.

Reading & Personal Reflection

Read the Scriptures and the devotional. Write down your first thoughts.

Ask yourself:
What part of this passage or reflection stands out most to me?

Where am I practicing joy?

Is there a part of me resisting or longing to connect with God right now?

_____
_____
_____
_____
_____
_____
_____
_____
_____
_____
_____
_____
_____

God of the flickering light,
 You are present in the chaos, the fear,
the uncertainty.

Teach me to notice the small sparks of joy You place along
my path — a laugh, a shared meal, a quie
moment of peace.

Even when life feels heavy, help me choose hope,
hold on to connection, and trust that You are near.

Let my heart resist despair and rest in the reminder
that joy is not the absence of trouble,
but Your presence within it.

Amen.

2

Contemplative Prayer

Sit quietly, breathe deeply, and read the prayer slowly. Pause to reflect, notice your thoughts and feelings, and rest in God's presence.

Deeper Reflection
Take a moment to dig deeper into these vereses and answer the questions below:

How does Scripture define joy in the midst of trials, and how is it different from happiness?

How can joy act as a spiritual tether to God, others, and life itself?

What is the relationship between perseverance and joy according to James 1:2–3?

How can we cultivate the intentional practice of joy in daily life, especially in the midst of suffering?

_____
_____
_____
_____
_____
_____
_____
_____
_____
_____
_____
_____
_____

Journal about a small flicker of joy you experienced this week despite challenges.

Reflect on what made it meaningful.

Create a short story or poem illustrating joy as a quiet light in the darkness.

Sketch, paint, or collage what joy looks like in your current season—tiny sparks, warm colors, or moments of connection.

Try a new creative practice as a rebellion against despair.

4

Creative Practice

Create something that helps you meditate on the Scripture and devotional

Community & Service

Invite a friend or neighbor into a small shared moment of joy—coffee, a walk, a conversation.

Send an encouraging note or text to someone who is struggling.
Invite someone to admire something beautiful with you whether that's art or music.

Reflect on ways you can intentionally cultivate moments of joy within your community or family this week.

_____
_____
_____
_____
_____
_____
_____
_____
_____
_____
_____
_____
_____

Find a quiet space and sit comfortably.

Close your eyes and breathe slowly. Imagine a flicker of light—joy—burning softly within your chest.

As you inhale, feel God's presence filling that space.

As you exhale, release fear, heaviness, or despair.

Rest in the reality that even small sparks of joy are evidence of God's nearness.

Let your soul linger in the assurance that joy can coexist with trials, and that choosing hope is a form of resistance against despair.

6
Rest Practice

All of our Parts

"You are fully known and fully loved, just as you are."

Psalm 139

"For the choir director: A psalm of David.

1 "O Lord, you have examined my heart

and know everything about me.

2 You know when I sit down or stand up.

You know my thoughts even when I'm far away.

3 You see me when I travel

and when I rest at home.

You know everything I do.

4 You know what I am going to say

even before I say it, Lord.

5 You go before me and follow me.

You place your hand of blessing on my head.

6 Such knowledge is too wonderful for me,

too great for me to understand!

7 I can never escape from your Spirit!

I can never get away from your presence!

8 If I go up to heaven, you are there;

if I go down to the grave,[a] you are there.

9 If I ride the wings of the morning,

if I dwell by the farthest oceans,

10 even there your hand will guide me,

and your strength will support me.

11 I could ask the darkness to hide me

and the light around me to become night—

12   but even in darkness I cannot hide from you.

To you the night shines as bright as day.

13 You made all the delicate, inner parts of my body

and knit me together in my mother's womb.

14 Thank you for making me so wonderfully complex!

Your workmanship is marvelous—how well I know it.

15 You watched me as I was being formed in utter seclusion, as I

was woven together in the dark of the womb.

16 You saw me before I was born.

Every day of my life was recorded in your book.

Every moment was laid out

before a single day had passed.

17 How precious are your thoughts about me, O God.

They cannot be numbered!

18 I can't even count them;

they outnumber the grains of sand!

And when I wake up,

you are still with me!

19 O God, if only you would destroy the wicked!

Get out of my life, you murderers!

20 They blaspheme you;

your enemies misuse your name.

21 O Lord, shouldn't I hate those who hate you?

Shouldn't I despise those who oppose you?

22 Yes, I hate them with total hatred,

for your enemies are my enemies.

23 Search me, O God, and know my heart;

test me and know my anxious thoughts.

24 Point out anything in me that offends you,

and lead me along the path of everlasting life."

Beloved, think about that for a moment. Every hidden thought, every conflicted feeling, every part of you—the critical voice, the fearful part, the joyful piece, the angry, messy fragments—God knows them all. He sees them, He hears them, and He is not shocked or disappointed.

As humans, we often try to hide the parts of ourselves that feel broken, chaotic, or contradictory. We present a polished version to the world, to friends, even to God. But the truth is, He already knows. Every fear, every shame, every "I don't know who I am right now" moment—He has counted them all.

In therapy, we talk about integrating the different parts of ourselves, recognizing and acknowledging them so that healing can happen. Spiritually, God invites us to do the same. He wants us to bring our whole selves to Him—not just the parts we think are acceptable, but the messy, complicated, tender, and conflicted pieces too.

There is freedom in this. When we stop hiding and start acknowledging the fullness of who we are, we begin to see ourselves as God sees us: wonderfully complex, deeply loved, and fully enough. The fractured, messy parts of you are not liabilities—they are pieces of the soul God is shaping, redeeming, and holding close.

So, today, bring every part of you to Him. Confess the hidden fears, the doubts, the chaos. Lift up the joyful, grateful, and hopeful pieces. And rest in the truth that God is intimately acquainted with all your ways. You are fully known and fully loved, just as you are.

Reading & Personal Reflection

Read the Scriptures and the devotional. Write down your first thoughts.

Ask yourself:
What part of this passage or reflection stands out most to me?

What parts of yourself are you hiding from God?

Is there a part of me resisting or longing to connect with God right now?

_____
_____
_____
_____
_____
_____
_____
_____
_____
_____
_____
_____
_____
_____

*O God, who searches the depths of my heart,
You know every fragment, every hidden thought,
every longing and fear.*

*I bring to You the messy, contradictory, and tender parts of
myself—the anxious, the joyful, the critical, the hopeful.*

Meet me here, in all that I am.

*Let me rest in Your gaze that neither judges nor
recoils, and hear Your gentle assurance that I
am fully known and fully loved.*

Amen.

2

Contemplative Prayer

Sit quietly, breathe deeply, and read the prayer slowly. Pause to reflect, notice your thoughts and feelings, and rest in God's presence.

3 Deeper Reflection

Take a moment to dig deeper into these vereses and answer the questions below:

How does God's intimate knowledge of us, as described in Psalm 139, challenge the ways we hide parts of ourselves from others or from Him?

What does it mean to bring "the messy, contradictory, and tender pieces" of ourselves before God?

How can understanding that God knows us completely shape our spiritual and emotional healing?

Journal about the parts of yourself you most often try to hide—what does it feel like to bring them before God?

Write a letter to God from the perspective of your most fearful or critical inner voice, letting Him respond in your writing.

Create a visual representation of yourself fully known—fragments, contradictions, and all—and meditate on God's love in that image.

4

Creative Practice

Create something that helps you meditate on the Scripture and devotional.

5 Community & Service

Share an honest part of your story with someone you trust, creating space for vulnerability and connection.

Offer support to someone struggling with self-judgment, shame, or hidden fears, modeling openness and acceptance.

Reflect on ways your own awareness of God's intimate knowledge can make you more empathetic and compassionate in community.

Find a quiet space and settle into a comfortable posture.

Close your eyes and breathe slowly, imagining God's gaze resting on every part of you—seen, hidden, and unresolved.

As you inhale, invite His presence into the spaces of fear, doubt, and chaos.

As you exhale, release the need to hide, perform, or fix yourself.

Let your soul rest in the truth that every fragment of your being is known and loved.

Rest in God's intimate care, letting the assurance of being fully known bring peace and freedom.

6

Rest Practice

The Growing Garden

"The good news is that God doesn't just tolerate the messy garden of our hearts—He tends it."

>

Psalm 92

"It is good to give thanks to the Lord,
  to sing praises to the Most High.
2 It is good to proclaim your unfailing love in the morning,
  your faithfulness in the evening,
3 accompanied by a ten-stringed instrument, a harp,
  and the melody of a lyre.
4 You thrill me, Lord, with all you have done for me!
  I sing for joy because of what you have done.
5 O Lord, what great works you do!
  And how deep are your thoughts.
6 Only a simpleton would not know,
  and only a fool would not understand this:
7 Though the wicked sprout like weeds
  and evildoers flourish,
  they will be destroyed forever.
8 But you, O Lord, will be exalted forever.
9 Your enemies, Lord, will surely perish;
  all evildoers will be scattered.
10 But you have made me as strong as a wild ox.
  You have anointed me with the finest oil.
11 My eyes have seen the downfall of my enemies;
  my ears have heard the defeat of my wicked opponents.
12 But the godly will flourish like palm trees
  and grow strong like the cedars of Lebanon.
13 For they are transplanted to the Lord's own house.
  They flourish in the courts of our God.
14 Even in old age they will still produce fruit;
  they will remain vital and green.
15 They will declare, "The Lord is just!
  He is my rock!
  There is no evil in him!""

"I am the true grapevine, and my Father is the gardener. 2 He cuts off every branch of mine that doesn't produce fruit, and he prunes the branches that do bear fruit so they will produce even more. 3 You have already been pruned and purified by the message I have given you. 4 Remain in me, and I will remain in you. For a branch cannot produce fruit if it is severed from the vine, and you cannot be fruitful unless you remain in me.
5 "Yes, I am the vine; you are the branches. Those who remain in me, and I in them, will produce much fruit. For apart from me you can do nothing. 6 Anyone who does not remain in me is thrown away like a useless branch and withers. Such branches are gathered into a pile to be burned. 7 But if you remain in me and my words remain in you, you may ask for anything you want, and it will be granted! 8 When you produce much fruit, you are my true disciples. This brings great glory to my Father. 9 "I have loved you even as the Father has loved me. Remain in my love. 10 When you obey my commandments, you remain in my love, just as I obey my Father's commandments and remain in his love. 11 I have told you these things so that you will be filled with my joy. Yes, your joy will overflow! 12 This is my commandment: Love each other in the same way I have loved you. 13 There is no greater love than to lay down one's life for one's friends. 14 You are my friends if you do what I command. 15 I no longer call you slaves, because a master doesn't confide in his slaves. Now you are my friends, since I have told you everything the Father told me. 16 You didn't choose me. I chose you. I appointed you to go and produce lasting fruit, so that the Father will give you whatever you ask for, using my name. 17 This is my command: Love each other."

John 15: 1- 17

There's a scene in The Shack that I think about often. Mack, the main character, is walking with Sarayu—the character who represents the Holy Spirit—through a garden described as "chaos in color." It's vibrant and wild and seemingly unkept. Mack looks around and says, "It's a mess." Sarayu smiles, taking it as a compliment.

She explains that from above, the garden forms a fractal—a complex and beautiful pattern that only makes sense when seen from a higher view. What looks chaotic up close is, in fact, very, very beautiful.

Later, Sarayu tells him, "This garden is your soul. This mess is you! Together, you and I, we have been working with a purpose in your heart. And it is wild and beautiful and perfectly in process. To you it seems like a mess, but to me, I see a perfect pattern emerging and growing and alive—a living fractal."

Many of us would probably admit that our inner lives feel very similar—part wonder, but mainly a mess. As a therapist, I've seen how early experiences—our upbringing, our relationships with caregivers, the stories we inherited—shape how we see God. Many of us live as though He's waiting to punish us, not delight in us. We walk around holding our breath, afraid our "mess" disqualifies us from love.

But that's not the Gospel. The good news is that God doesn't just tolerate the messy garden of our hearts—He tends it. He walks through it with gentleness and joy. Even in suffering, He's weeding what chokes life,
pruning what no longer serves growth, and cultivating what will one day bloom into holiness.

Maybe right now, your life looks less like a well-kept garden and more like chaos in color. Maybe you can't yet see the pattern taking shape. But the Gardener can. He looks at your soul and says, "Wow. What a beautiful sight. What a joy it is to know and be with My child."

Reading & Personal Reflection

Read the Scriptures and the devotional. Write down your first thoughts.

Ask yourself:
What part of this passage or reflection stands out most to me?

What part of your inner life do you tend to label as "a mess"?

Is there a part of me resisting or longing to connect with God right now?

_____
_____
_____
_____
_____
_____
_____
_____
_____
_____
_____
_____
_____

*O Gardener of my soul,
You see the wild, chaotic colors of my heart.*

*Where I see disorder, You see fractals of beauty,
patterns I cannot yet discern.*

Walk with me through the tangled paths and unkempt corners.

Tend my heart with patience, prune what stifles growth, cultivate what will bloom.

Teach me to trust Your eye, Your timing, and Your delight in me.

Let me flourish in Your courts, even in the midst of my own mess.

Amen.

2

Contemplative Prayer

Sit quietly, breathe deeply, and read the prayer slowly. Pause to reflect, notice your thoughts and feelings, and rest in God's presence.

Deeper Reflection
Take a moment to dig deeper into these vereses and answer the questions below:

How does John 15:5 describe the relationship between abiding in Christ and bearing fruit?

What does Psalm 92 teach us about flourishing over a lifetime, even in seasons of chaos or difficulty?

In what ways does God actively cultivate and tend the garden of our souls, even when we cannot see the pattern?

_____
_____
_____
_____
_____
_____
_____
_____
_____
_____
_____
_____
_____
_____

Read this quote:

"Imagine yourself as a living house. God comes in to rebuild that house. At first, perhaps, you can understand what He is doing. He is getting the drains right and stopping the leaks in the roof and so on; you knew that those jobs needed doing and so you are not surprised. But presently He starts knocking the house about in a way that hurts abominably and does not seem to make any sense. What on earth is He up to? The explanation is that He is building quite a different house from the one you thought of - throwing out a new wing here, putting on an extra floor there, running up towers, making courtyards. You thought you were being made into a decent little cottage: but He is building a palace. He intends to come and live in it Himself."

- C.S. Lewis, Mere Christianity

Take a moment to visualize your inner self as a house. What does it look like right now? Are there rooms that feel broken, cluttered, or abandoned? Which spaces feel vibrant, alive, or full of light?
Now, imagine God walking through this house. He touches each corner with care. He repairs what is broken, clears what is stagnant, and paints walls with new color. He keeps the heart of the house intact, but strengthens and beautifies it in ways only He can.

Using any medium you like—pencil, pen, watercolor, collage—draw your inner house. Include the parts that feel messy, the spaces that bring you joy, and the rooms that are under construction.

Don't worry about artistic skill; focus on expressing what's happening in your soul.

4
Creative Practice
Create something that helps you meditate on the Scripture and devotional.

Community & Service

Serve at a local nonprofit serving people who are different than you.

Help in a community garden, church garden, or school garden.

Offer guidance, care, or mentorship to someone who is learning to trust God's work in their life.

Reflect on ways your own flourishing can serve as an example of God's patient, creative work to others.

Find a quiet space and breathe slowly, imagining yourself as a garden under God's care.

As you inhale, feel His presence filling every tangled corner of your heart.

As you exhale, release judgment, shame, and the desire to control growth.

Rest in the truth that even the chaos of your life is under His watchful eye, and that the Gardener delights in what is wild, vibrant, and alive in you.

6
Rest Practice

Arms Held Up

"Suffering becomes an invitation—to be held by others, and through them, to be reminded that God is near."

> "While the people of Israel were still at Rephidim, the warriors of Amalek attacked them. 9 Moses commanded Joshua, "Choose some men to go out and fight the army of Amalek for us. Tomorrow, I will stand at the top of the hill, holding the staff of God in my hand." 10 So Joshua did what Moses had commanded and fought the army of Amalek. Meanwhile, Moses, Aaron, and Hur climbed to the top of a nearby hill. 11 As long as Moses held up the staff in his hand, the Israelites had the advantage. But whenever he dropped his hand, the Amalekites gained the advantage. 12 Moses' arms soon became so tired he could no longer hold them up. So Aaron and Hur found a stone for him to sit on. Then they stood on each side of Moses, holding up his hands. So his hands held steady until sunset. 13 As a result, Joshua overwhelmed the army of Amalek in battle.
> 14 After the victory, the Lord instructed Moses, "Write this down on a scroll as a permanent reminder, and read it aloud to Joshua: I will erase the memory of Amalek from under heaven." 15 Moses built an altar there and named it Yahweh-Nissi (which means "the Lord is my banner"). 16 He said, "They have raised their fist against the Lord's throne, so now[c] the Lord will be at war with Amalek generation after generation."

Exodus 17:8-16

One of my favorite Old Testament stories is found in Exodus 17, during Israel's battle with the Amalekites. Whenever Moses held up his arms with God's staff, Israel prevailed. But whenever he lowered them, the Amalekites began to win. Over time, Moses grew tired.

So Aaron and Hur brought him a stone to sit on, and they stood beside him—each one supporting one of his hands. Scripture says, "So his hands were steady until the sun set." And because of this, Israel won the battle.

It's such a curious and beautiful passage. First, it reminds us that it is God who fights and wins the battles. Israel's victory had nothing to do with their own strength but everything to do with God's sovereignty and goodness toward His people.

But there's another layer here—a quiet lesson about community. The text doesn't linger on Aaron and Hur's actions, yet their role is profound. Moses' victory depended not only on God's power but also on the willingness of his community to hold him up. Sometimes, as believers, it's easier to trust that God will come through than it is to let others come close enough to help us.

Yes, the battle belongs to the Lord. And yet, there is a real humanity here—a picture of what it means to need others even as we walk in obedience to God. In seasons of suffering, it can be hard to let people see us in our weariness. But research—and Scripture—both tell us that one of the most transformative experiences in life is to be seen and known. Real change, real healing, often happens within the context of human relationships.

What's striking is that God could have easily given Moses supernatural strength. We know the staff itself wasn't the source of power—it was merely symbolic. And still, God didn't allow Moses to do it alone. I imagine Moses, weary on the mountain. His arms heavy as the sun beat down. The battle raging below. And God, in all His power, doesn't remove the burden or infuse Moses with instant endurance. Instead, He sends Aaron and Hur. Two friends. Two steady hands. A stone for rest.

God knew Moses' exhaustion—and He made space for it. He met it through the quiet, ordinary help of others.
I wonder how many times we miss the work God wants to do in us because we refuse to let others hold up our arms. Sometimes that support looks like intercessory prayer. Sometimes it's a hot meal, a funny meme, or a hard conversation that helps us face what's really in our hearts.

Suffering becomes an invitation—to be held by others, and through them, to be reminded that God is near.

Reading & Personal Reflection

Read the Scriptures and the devotional. Write down your first thoughts.

Ask yourself:
What part of this passage or reflection stands out most to me?

Who is currently helping you hold your arms up?

Is there a part of me resisting or longing to connect with God right now?

_____
_____
_____
_____
_____
_____
_____
_____
_____
_____
_____
_____
_____
_____

O God, who fights for Your people, I lift my weary hands to You, and yet the weight of life presses down.

Be near to me in my exhaustion, and send steady hands to support me.

Teach me to receive help without shame, to trust in the presence of others, and to let Your love flow through human care as well as divine power.

May I be both held and holding, in Your grace.

Amen.

2
Contemplative Prayer
Sit quietly, breathe deeply, and read the prayer slowly. Pause to reflect, notice your thoughts and feelings, and rest in God's presence.

Deeper Reflection
Take a moment to dig deeper into these vereses and answer the questions below:

How does the story of Moses, Aaron, and Hur illustrate the interplay between God's power and human community?

What does it mean that God allows Moses to be weary instead of giving him instant supernatural strength?

How can suffering become a context in which we are held by others and experience God's nearness?

How can we cultivate humility to receive help and courage to offer it to others?

_____
_____
_____
_____
_____
_____
_____
_____
_____
_____
_____

Reflect in your journal about a season when someone held you up—how did that support help you persevere?

Draw or write about what "steady hands" look like in your life right now—friends, family, mentors, or even God's Spirit.

Write a letter of gratitude to someone who has been a steady presence in your life.

4

Creative Practice

Create something that helps you meditate on the Scripture and devotional.

Community & Service

Reach out to someone in your circle who is weary, and ask how you can help suppor them.

Pray for a friend or community member who is in a spiritual or emotional battle.

Offer your time, attention, or presence to someone struggling.

Write letters of gratitude to those who have supported you.

_____
_____
_____
_____
_____
_____
_____
_____
_____
_____
_____
_____
_____
_____

Find a quiet place and close your eyes. Visualize your weary hands lifted toward God.

As you inhale, sense God's presence surrounding you.

As you exhale, release the need to carry burdens alone.

Picture Aaron and Hur standing beside you, holding your hands steady.

Let yourself rest in the truth that God's victory often flows through community, and that being held is a sacred part of walking in obedience to Him.

6

Rest Practice

The Ending That Can't Be Undone

"We will be held in the deepest relationship with Him. And we will live—finally and fully—without sorrow, shame, or condemnation as His beloved Child."

>

"Then I saw a new heaven and a new earth, for the old heaven and the old earth had disappeared. And the sea was also gone. 2 And I saw the holy city, the new Jerusalem, coming down from God out of heaven like a bride beautifully dressed for her husband. 3 I heard a loud shout from the throne, saying, "Look, God's home is now among his people! He will live with them, and they will be his people. God himself will be with them. 4 He will wipe every tear from their eyes, and there will be no more death or sorrow or crying or pain. All these things are gone forever." 5 And the one sitting on the throne said, "Look, I am making everything new!" And then he said to me, "Write this down, for what I tell you is trustworthy and true." 6 And he also said, "It is finished! I am the Alpha and the Omega—the Beginning and the End. To all who are thirsty I will give freely from the springs of the water of life. 7 All who are victorious will inherit all these blessings, and I will be their God, and they will be my children."

Revelation 21: 1-7

"But now, O Jacob, listen to the Lord who created you.
   O Israel, the one who formed you says,
"Do not be afraid, for I have ransomed you.
   I have called you by name; you are mine.
2 When you go through deep waters,
   I will be with you.
When you go through rivers of difficulty,
   you will not drown.
When you walk through the fire of oppression,
   you will not be burned up;
   the flames will not consume you.

3 For I am the Lord, your God,
   the Holy One of Israel, your Savior.
I gave Egypt as a ransom for your freedom;
   I gave Ethiopia[a] and Seba in your place.
4 Others were given in exchange for you.
   I traded their lives for yours
because you are precious to me.
   You are honored, and I love you."

Isaiah 43: 1-4

God is completely capable of repairing, redeeming, and restoring everything we have ever lost. He can heal every rupture, cure every ailment, and mend every heart. We rejoice and thank Him for the ways He shows up in our everyday lives. He cares so deeply for us, and He is always moving on our behalf—whether or not we see it or feel it.

But as long as we live on this fallen earth, we will feel the tension of decay, longing, and ache. We know—deep in our bones—that the world is not as it should be. We feel it in our personal lives, we see it in the news, and we scroll past it daily on our screens. So we live in the tension of the "already and the not yet." We catch glimpses of Him in our children's faces, hear Him in our father's laughter, feel Him in a fall breeze—yet we recognize these are only shadows of what's to come.

C.S. Lewis describes this longing so well:

"If I find in myself a desire which no experience in this world can satisfy, the most probable explanation is that I was made for another world... Earthly pleasures were never meant to satisfy it, but only to arouse it, to suggest the real thing... I must keep alive in myself the desire for my true country... and make it the main object of life to press on to that other country and to help others do the same."

He is speaking of our truest home—the new heaven and the new earth—where we will dwell with God. My intention is not to dampen hope but to lift our eyes toward the greater Hope... the ending that cannot be undone, the world as it will be when He sets all things right.

Read this aloud:

"Look, God's home is now among His people! He will live with me, and I will be His. God Himself will be with me. He will wipe every tear from my eyes, and there will be no more death or sorrow or crying or pain. All these things are gone forever."

Say it again:

"All these things are gone FOREVER."

Beloved, our suffering does have an end. God Himself will end every form of grief, death, and pain—and once He does, it cannot be undone. So we hold tightly to this hope: that no matter what happens on this side of heaven, we will be with Him forever. We will be our truest selves in His presence. We will be held in the
deepest relationship with Him. And we will live—finally and fully—without sorrow, shame, or condemnation as His beloved Child.

Reading & Personal Reflection

Read the Scriptures and the devotional. Write down your first thoughts.

Ask yourself:
What part of this passage or reflection stands out most to me?

What part of me struggles to trust this future hope?

What part of me clings to it?

Is there a part of me resisting or longing to connect with God right now?

_____
_____
_____
_____
_____
_____
_____
_____
_____
_____
_____
_____
_____

God who makes all things new,
You hold every tear I've cried and every sorrow
I cannot name.

You see what has been lost, what has broken,
what still aches.

Yet You promise a day when death will be no more, when
grief and pain will be undone forever.

Until that day, be my comfort, my steady ground, my Holy
Presence in the in-between.

Help me trust the story You are still writing—one where
redemption has the final word.

Amen.

2

Contemplative Prayer

Sit quietly, breathe deeply, and read the prayer slowly. Pause to reflect, notice your thoughts and feelings, and rest in God's presence.

Deeper Reflection
Take a moment to dig deeper into these vereses and answer the questions below:

Revelation 21 says God's home is now among His people. What does it mean to you that God chooses to dwell with us, even in our unfinished or painful seasons?

The passage promises "no more death or sorrow, crying or pain." How does this eternal promise reshape how you view current struggles?

What do the images of a new heaven, new earth, and God wiping every tear reveal about His character, tenderness, and intentions towards humanity?

___
___
___
___
___
___
___
___
___
___
___
___
___
___
___

Draw or paint an image of your current "middle place," including both the ache and glimpses of God's presence.

Write a letter to yourself from God's perspective, affirming His faithfulness and nearness in your unfinished story.

Create art using the imagery of "new heavens," "new earth," or "no more tears."

4

Creative Practice

Create something that helps you meditate on the Scripture and devotional.

Community & Service

Reach out to someone who is enduring a long season of uncertainty or grief. Offer prayer, a message of encouragement, or practical support.

Consider a practical act of love: Send a handwritten note, drop off a meal, sit with them, or simply say, "I'm here with you."

If appropriate, share a story of hope or God's faithfulness with someone struggling, demonstrating presence over solution.

Find a quiet place. Close your eyes and place your hands gently on your lap or chest.

Inhale slowly, and imagine God gathering your tears -every one.

Exhale and imagine Him lifting the burden of sorry from your shoulders.

With each breath, whisper a phrase:
Inhale: "He sees."
Exhale: "He will restore."

Visualize His nearness in your current struggles, as if He is beside you holding your hands.

Stay here for several minutes. Let your whole being rest in this truth: The story ends in restoration.

6

Rest Practice

Acknowledgements

First, to my husband, Anthony. You didn't just help me format and publish this book—you have been my steady anchor through every storm. Thank you for staying beside me while I stayed up late writing, reflecting, dreaming, and wrestling with words.

To my parents and brother: thank you for always believing in me. To Sony, my sister, thank you for your unwavering love and presence. To Randy, my editor and sandwich maker extraordinaire amongst other things: I will never go hungry because of you.

To Alejandra and Meagan, my friends who lifted my hands when I could no longer hold them: thank you for letting me cry on your couch, for sharing meals and laughter, and for the long, late-night texts that reminded me I was not alone.

To Juliana, thank you for being a constant and a safe space to land with all parts of my humanity. I will never be able to thank you for how you held me when the world felt upside down.

To my therapist, Lindsay, thank you for walking with me through the dark, messy seasons, for asking the hard questions, and for guiding me toward God even when I couldn't see Him clearly. Your wisdom, presence, and encouragement shaped this book more than words can capture.

To my coworkers and my clients: thank you for showing me, every day, the courage it takes to live with grace in the midst of life's challenges. Your resilience inspires me, and your stories remind me why I do this work. As a therapist, I often sit with people navigating pain I cannot fix—but your willingness to show up and endure has taught me more about faith, hope, and trust than any lesson I could have studied.

And above all, to Jesus. You are my anchor, my refuge, my safe place. You have not only saved my life—you have transformed it. You held me, reshaped me, and called me into a fullness I could never reach on my own.

You are worthy. Always worthy.

Made in the USA
Coppell, TX
20 January 2026

68900129R00096